Next Steps in
altered
photo
ARTISTRY

New Ways to Transform Images for Fabric & Quilt Art

BETH WHEELER

Acknowledgments

This book would not be possible without the
constant support of my family, loved ones, and friends:
My loving husband, Geoff; my mom and number-one
cheerleader, Ellie Ferguson; my incredible son, Jake; my
late father, Walter Johnson (who always encouraged
me to be the best I could possibly be); and of course
Lori Marquette, my studio partner who cheerfully
follows me into battle, waving the "What if?" flag. Lori
coordinated the add-ons so I could focus on writing
the book.

My heartfelt appreciation and respect are also
extended to the wonderful crew at C&T Publishing:
Amy Marson, publisher; Kesel Wilson, developmental
editor; Zinnia Heinzmann, technical editor; and
Kerry Graham, designer.

I'd also like to thank the generous quilt artists who
read our first book with C&T Publishing, *Altered Photo
Artistry*, then made quilts using my techniques and
shared them with me in this book.

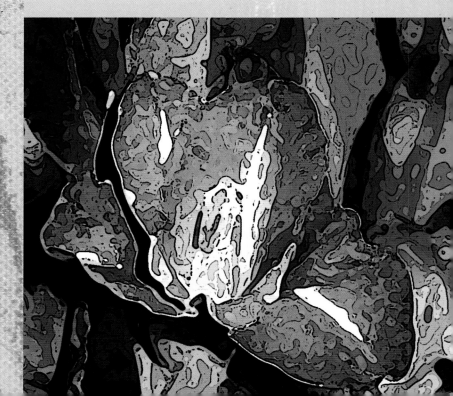

contents

Introduction

After the publication of my first book with C&T Publishing, *Altered Photo Artistry,* it became apparent that quilters are indeed quite computer savvy. They want more information about altering their own photographs and are undaunted by the software applications that make it possible. My hat goes off to them and their adventurous spirit!

This book is filled to the brim with exercises and tips for making the most of popular photo-editing software. I've focused on Adobe Photoshop Elements 6 (PSE 6) because it is available for both PC and Mac platforms, is reasonably priced, and is user-friendly. Adobe is continually upgrading the software to make the features even more efficient. The tools may be grouped or located differently from version to version, but they function the same today as they did when the first version of Photoshop 1 was introduced years ago.

Thank you for joining me in another remarkable adventure using the computer and inkjet printer as quilting tools. Enjoy!

Beth Wheeler

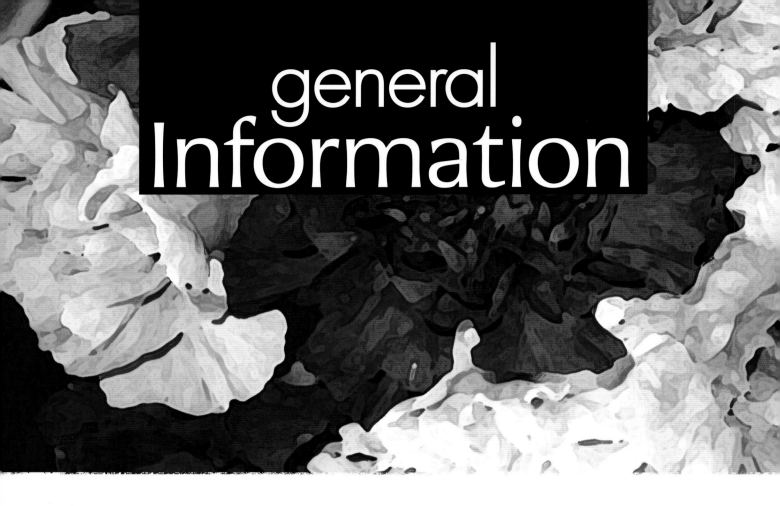

general Information

Things to Note

- All instructions in the book are written for Adobe Photoshop Elements 6 (PSE 6) for Windows.

- All screen captures (photos of the computer screen) are from PSE 6 for Windows.

- Keyboard shortcuts are written for Windows. If you have a Mac, simply substitute Command (⌘) for Control (Ctrl) and Option for Alt.

Finding Tools

Throughout the exercises in this book, you may come across a tool that is not readily available in your Toolbox at the left of the screen. Often, these tools are nested behind a similar type of tool. To access these "hidden" tools, simply click on the small black triangle at the bottom right of one of the tool icons and choose from the pop-up menu. This example shows the Selection Brush tool nested behind the Quick Selection tool.

bonus CD

The bonus CD in the back of the book contains my own add-ons, such as displacement maps, brushes, and textures, developed over many years of experimentation, as well as step-by-step instructions for loading the add-ons into Adobe Photoshop Elements. Also included are all of the original photos and images shown in this book, a bonus copy of the "Printing Photos on Fabric" chapter from my first book with C&T Publishing, *Altered Photo Artistry*, and a free limited feature trial version of Adobe Photoshop Elements for PC.

Navigating Photoshop Elements

The main window in Photoshop Elements contains many different sections. Whether you're new to Photoshop Elements or not, review the image below to get to know the names and functions of each area.

PHOTOSHOP ELEMENTS MAIN WINDOW

- **Toolbox** The Toolbox contains the basic editing tools.

- **Options bar** The Options bar displays the settings of a selected tool.

- **Project bin** The Project bin shows a thumbnail of each file that is open.

- **Palette bin** The Palette bin contains various palettes, such as Layers and Effects.

- **Layers palette** The Layers palette displays all layers of an open file.

- **Effects palette** The Effects palette provides shortcuts to filters, layer styles, and photo effects.

- **Menu bar** The Menu bar contains all of the functions available in Photoshop Elements.

- **Workspace** The workspace contains all open files.

The instructions in this book are written in shorthand to efficiently direct you to files, folders, and menu choices. For example, **Image > Resize > Image Size** means: "Go to the menu bar at the top of the screen and click on **Image**. From that menu, choose the **Resize** option and click on **Image Size** from the pop-up menu."

Likewise, when you see keyboard shortcuts such as Alt+Ctrl+I, it means: "Hold down the Alt and Control keys while pressing the I key." This example is a shortcut to the Image Size menu.

Path to Image Size

Standard Commands

Undo and Undo History

If you change your mind or make a mistake at any point, simply choose **Edit > Undo** or press Ctrl+Z. This will reverse the last action applied to the image. If you'd like to redo anything you just undid, choose **Edit > Redo** or press Ctrl+Y.

If you need to back up several steps, open the Undo History palette by choosing **Window > Undo History.** This palette contains a list of every action applied to the image since it was opened. Clicking on any item will cause the image to revert to that point.

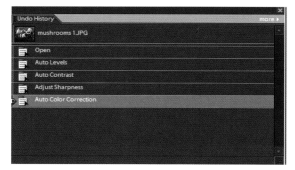

Undo History palette

Optimize

Many photo imperfections can be fixed using the auto-correction tools in Photoshop Elements. Click on **Enhance** in the top menu bar. From this menu you can choose to apply **Auto Smart Fix**, **Auto Levels**, **Auto Contrast**, **Auto Color Correction**, **Auto Sharpen**, and **Auto Red Eye Fix** to your photo, one at a time.

By default, Photoshop Elements saves 50 steps in the Undo History palette. To adjust this number, go to **Edit > Preferences > Performance > History & Cache.** You can increase this number to a maximum of 1,000 steps, but be aware that saving a large number of steps may slow down your system.

Save As

When you are pleased with the image, save two copies: one Photoshop (PSD) file with layers retained for future editing, and one TIFF file with flattened layers for printing.

1. Open the Save As dialog box: Choose **File > Save As** or press Ctrl+Shift+S. Give the file a unique name (something different from the original file) and select Photoshop (.psd) from the Format pull-down menu. Click the Layers checkbox to retain any layers and press Save. This copy of the file is for future editing.

Save as a Photoshop file (.psd) for future editing.

2. Flatten your file: Choose **Layer > Flatten**. Open the Save As dialog box again (Ctrl+Shift+S) to save a second copy of the file. Keep the file location and name the same. Select TIFF (.tif) from the Format pull-down menu and press Save. This copy of the file is for printing.

Cropping

1. <u>Select the area to be cropped</u>: Select the Marquee tool, or press M, and click and drag a box around the area of the image you'd like to keep. When you release the mouse button you should see "marching ants" around the edge of the selected area. You can reposition the marquee by clicking inside the box and dragging it. If you make a mistake, go to **Select > Deselect** or press Ctrl+D to erase the box and start over.

OR

<u>Set a fixed size to be cropped:</u> If you want to set a fixed size for the marquee, simply select Fixed Size from the Mode menu in the Options bar and enter your settings into the Width and Height boxes. Reposition the marquee as you wish with the cursor.

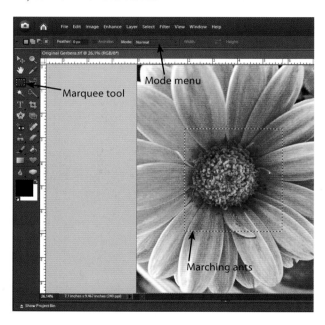

2. <u>Crop the image:</u> Go to **Image > Crop** to cut off the unwanted area and press Ctrl+D to deselect the marquee.

Resizing an Image

Before you resize an image, it's important to consider whether the image will be printed (for an Altered Photo quilt, for example) or viewed on screen (in an email, blog, or website). No matter what the end result is, the goal in downsampling (reducing) or upsampling (enlarging) an image is to change the size *without* degrading the quality of the image.

To get started, let's open the Image Size dialog box and review the two main sections. Go to **Image > Resize > Image Size** (Alt+Ctrl+I).

- The Pixel Dimensions section tells how many *pixels* wide and tall the image is. You will use this section of the dialog box when preparing an image for on-screen viewing.

- The Document Size section refers to document size and current resolution. It tells how many *inches* wide and tall the image is and how many pixels per inch the resolution is. You will use this section of the dialog box when preparing an image for printing.

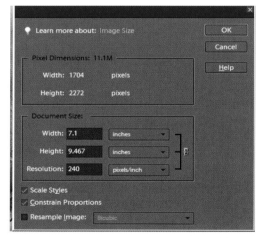

Image Size dialog box

Note

Resolution can be destroyed, but not created. When you decrease the resolution of an image, you're deleting pixels. When you increase the resolution of an image, you're stretching the pixels, not adding them. It's important to realize that you cannot increase the resolution of an image beyond its original size from the camera or scanner.

For On-Screen Viewing

1. Set the resolution to 72 pixels per inch (ppi): With the Image Size dialog box open (Alt+Ctrl+I), make sure the Resample Image box is unchecked and set the resolution to 72 ppi. Because the resolution of most monitors is 72 ppi, setting the resolution of our image to match this number gives us a better idea of the actual on-screen size of our image when we change the pixel dimensions in the next step.

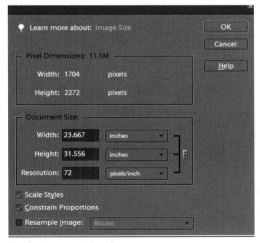

Resolution set to 72 ppi

2. Resize the image: Click the Resample Image box to turn it on, and make sure that the Constrain Proportions box is checked. In the Pixel Dimensions section, set one side (either the width or the height) to no more than 650 pixels. The dimension for the other side automatically updates proportionally. You can review and adjust the actual on-screen size of the image in the Document Size section, as long as the pixel dimension for either side remains below 650. Click OK to resize the image.

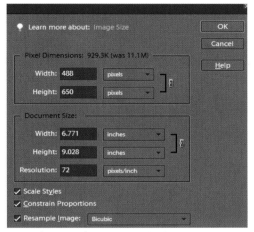

Resize the image for on-screen viewing.

3. Save your work: When you are pleased with the image, go to **File > Save for Web** (Alt+Shift+Ctrl+S) to optimize and save it for on-screen viewing (see Saving for the Web, page 11).

Resizing for an Altered Photo Quilt

The standard Altered Photo quilt size is 8" × 10½" or multiples of that ratio: 16" × 21" for a 2 × 2; 24" × 31½" for a 3 × 3; or 32" × 42" for a 4 × 4.

For Printing

In general, the higher the resolution, the better the image will be when printed on fabric or paper. For the best-quality prints, fabric requires 150 ppi, and paper requires between 200 and 300 ppi.

1. Review the resolution: With the Image Size dialog box open (Alt+Ctrl+I), make sure the Resample Image box is unchecked and review the resolution in the Document Size section. If the resolution is not within the ideal ppi range (see For Printing, above), set the correct ppi in the Resolution box and review the updated image dimensions in the Document Size section. If you're happy with the image size, click OK and go to Step 3.

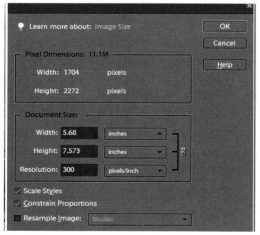

Resolution set to 300 ppi with Resample Image box unchecked

2. Make further adjustments: If you need to further adjust the image dimensions, click OK and crop the image to the desired size (see Cropping, page 8). Return to the Image Size dialog box (Alt+Ctrl+I) and click the Resample Image box to turn it on. Choose Bicubic Smoother or Sharper from the Resample Image pull-down menu and click OK (see Resampling Tip, below).

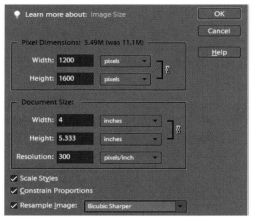

Resolution set to 300 ppi with Resample Image box checked

3. Save your work: When you are pleased with the image, go to **File > Save As** (Ctrl+Shift+S) to save the image as a separate file from the original (see Save As, page 7).

If you find yourself upsampling many photos to print on fabric or paper, you may want to consider a more sophisticated third-party plug-in program for better results (see Resources section, page 79).

Saving for the Web

Photoshop Elements makes it easy to reduce the size of any photo and save it in a format that is convenient to upload, download, and view on the Internet.

Save for Web dialog box

1. Resize the image: Resize your image for on-screen viewing (see For On-Screen Viewing, page 9).

2. Select the file format: Open the Save for Web dialog box by choosing **File > Save for Web** or press Alt+Shift+Ctrl+S. Select JPEG High from the Preset pull-down menu and click OK.

3. Save your work: Enter a unique name and destination for the optimized image and click Save.

Computer
Effects

See Book 1, *Altered Photo Artistry*, for the following topics:

Photography Equipment & Supplies:

- Pretreated Fabrics
- Home-Treated Fabrics
- Inkjet Printers
- Inks
- Photos & Digital Art

- Computers & Scanners
- Digital Cameras
- Photo-Editing Software
- Printing on Fabric FAQs

4-Block Layout

In this exercise we'll create four altered versions of a photograph for a sample 4-block Altered Photo quilt using four color and textural variations of the same image. The original photo should be in color, have an obvious focal point, and have good contrast between the foreground and background. Choose a floral, landscape, still life, or architectural subject, and save portraits of people and animals for another day.

Finished 4-block layout

Original pink canna photo (Canna.jpg)

Prepare the Image

1. Open the pink canna photo: Open the image in Photoshop Elements by choosing **File > Open** (Ctrl+O). Navigate to Canna.jpg on the CD, select it, and click OK.

2. Optimize the image: Refer to Optimize, page 6, to adjust color, lighting, and sharpness using the auto-correction tools. If you don't like the result, simply **Undo** the changes (Ctrl+Z).

3. Resize the image: Because the altered images will be printed for a 4-block Altered Photo quilt, enlarge or reduce and crop the photo to 8″ × 10½″ (see the For Printing section of Resizing an Image, page 10).

4. Save your work: When you are pleased with the image, go to **File > Save As** (Ctrl+Shift+S) to save the image as a separate file from the original (see Save As, page 7). This file will be the starting point for all four of your altered photos in this exercise.

Explore Artistic Filters

Some of the most powerful artistic tools in Photoshop Elements are found in the filter gallery.

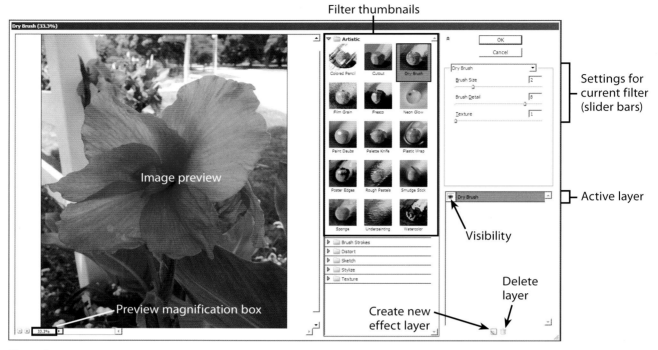

Filter gallery

1. <u>Open the filter gallery</u>: With the optimized canna photo open from Step 4 of Prepare the Image, page 13, go to **Filter > Filter Gallery**.

2. <u>Click on the thumbnail of the desired tool</u>: A preview window and a control panel with slider bars will appear. Before experimenting with the control sliders, make sure a critical portion of the image is visible in the preview window. Adjust the percentage in the preview magnification box and use the navigation bars along the side and bottom to display an important area of the image. Or fit the entire image in the preview window by pressing Ctrl+zero.

3. <u>Experiment</u>: Play with the various effects by moving the control sliders back and forth (see A Closer Look at Filters, page 16, for examples of filter effects). Review the results in the preview window. If you don't like the effect, select **Undo** (Ctrl+Z) and try again.

For more variety, try applying multiple filters to your image. Click the square icon at the bottom of the Layers section to add a new effect layer (see the filter gallery, above). Choose a new filter and adjust the settings as you like.

4. <u>Save your work</u>: When you are pleased with the image, go to **File > Save As** (Ctrl+Shift+S) to save the image as a separate file from the original (see Save As, page 7).

5. Repeat Steps 1–4 until you have four altered canna photos.

Make Final Adjustments

1. <u>Print comparisons on paper</u>: Print each of the four altered canna photos on individual sheets of paper. Print at normal print quality; there is no need to waste ink on high-quality prints at this time. Lay each printout on a tabletop or floor, and evaluate not only the look of each individually, but also the way they interact with one another.

Four finalists; these were chosen because the textures contrast, yet look nice together: Fresco, Poster Edges, Sponge, Cutout filters.

Four finalists with color.

2. Adjust the color: Make adjustments to each of the four altered canna photos separately by opening the Hue/Saturation dialog box. Go to **Enhance > Adjust Color > Adjust Hue/Saturation** (Ctrl+U). Move the slider bars to adjust the color. Click OK to apply the changes.

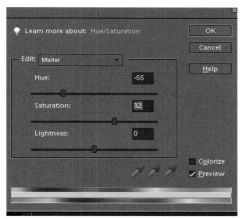

Experiment with control slider bars.

3. Save your work: When you are pleased with the changes to each image, go to **File > Save As** (Ctrl+Shift+S) to save the image as a separate file from the original (see Save As, page 7).

4. Compare the adjusted images: Print each of the four adjusted images at normal quality and reevaluate the composition. Continue making adjustments until you get the look you want.

Additional Examples

Poppies, 12″ × 12″, by Georgianne Kandler, Arroyo Grande, California

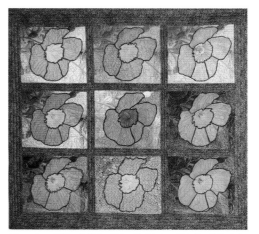

Blooming, 39″ × 31″, by Priscilla Stultz, Fairfax, Virginia

A Closer Look at Filters

There are dozens of filters in Photoshop Elements. Below are samples and settings for 15 of my favorite filters. Remember: Any filter may be applied to the image more than once—or apply one filter on top of another for endless altering effects.

COLORED PENCIL

Colored pencil filter; for dramatic results, set pencil width to 6, stroke pressure to 15, and paper brightness to 50.

DRY BRUSH

Dry brush filter; control sliders set at brush size 10, brush detail 10, and texture 3.

CUTOUT FILTER

Cutout filter; for maximum drama and details, set levels to 8, edge simplicity to 0, and edge fidelity to 3.

FILM GRAIN

Film grain filter; control sliders set at grain 7, highlight area 4, and intensity 10. This filter looks great when applied to rasterized text.

FRESCO

Fresco filter; control sliders set at brush size 10, brush detail 3, and texture 3. This filter looks best on light images.

PAINT DAUBS

Paint daubs filter; the brush style is set to wide sharp.

NEON GLOW

Neon glow filter; control sliders set at glow size 9 and glow brightness 22. This filter creates an odd but cool effect.

PALETTE KNIFE

Palette knife filter; control sliders set to stroke size 28, stroke detail 3, and softness 0. This filter looks best when applied in addition to other filters, such as Emboss.

PLASTIC WRAP

Plastic wrap filter; control sliders set to highlight strength 15, detail 9, and smoothness 7. This filter doesn't resonate with everyone, but it may become your favorite!

ROUGH PASTELS

Rough pastels filter; control sliders set to stroke length 17, stroke detail 18, burlap texture, 200% scaling, relief 50, bottom light, and Invert box checked.

POSTER EDGES

Poster edges filter; control sliders set to edge thickness 10, edge intensity 5, and posterization 6. This filter can be fabulous or blah, depending on the original image.

SMUDGE STICK

Smudge stick filter; control sliders set to stroke length 10, highlight area 7, and intensity 10.

SPONGE

Sponge filter; control sliders set to brush size 10, definition 25, and smoothness 4. This filter has an interesting texture that looks great with free-motion stitching.

UNDERPAINTING

Underpainting filter; control sliders set to brush size 33, texture coverage 40, texture brick, scaling 200%, relief 50, top light, and Invert box unchecked.

WATERCOLOR

Watercolor filter; control sliders set to brush detail 14, shadow intensity 1, and texture 3.

Square-in-a-Square

One way to create a larger image from a low-resolution photo is to place the image at its best quality on top of an enlarged, screened-back version of it. This controls where the eye goes (to the best-quality image), but carries color, texture, and theme through the overall composition.

Original gerbera daisy photo (Gerbera.jpg)

Finished square-in-a-square

Instructions

1. <u>Open and optimize the image</u>: See Prepare the Image, page 13, for instructions on opening and optimizing the image. Navigate to Gerbera.jpg on the CD, select it, and click OK.

2. <u>Duplicate the image twice</u>: Make three total copies of the image. Go to **Edit > Duplicate Layer** (Ctrl+J). You will now have a Layer 1 copy, a Layer 1, and a Background layer.

Layers window with duplicated layers

3. Reset the default for foreground and background colors: With the *Background layer selected*, click the tiny box in the lower left-hand corner of the Toolbox to reset the background color to white and the foreground color to black. This will be applied only to the specific layer you have selected.

Reset foreground and background color

4. Delete the Background layer: With the *Background layer still selected*, press Ctrl+A to select all and press delete. The Background layer should now be white in the Layers palette.

Background deleted

5. Apply High Pass to the Layer 1 copy: With the *Layer 1 copy selected*, go to **Filter > Other > High Pass**. In the dialog box, set the radius to 15.7 pixels and click OK.

High Pass dialog box

6. Apply the Film Grain filter to the Layer 1 copy: With the *Layer 1 copy still selected*, go to **Filter > Artistic > Film Grain**. In the dialog box, set the grain to 0, highlight area to 18, and intensity to 10. Click OK.

Film grain filter applied to image

7. Increase the contrast of the Layer 1 copy: With the *Layer 1 copy still selected*, go to **Enhance > Adjust Lighting > Brightness/Contrast**. Increase the contrast by about 50% to define the outline.

8. Make Layer 1 invisible: Click the eye icon to the left of Layer 1 (the layer with color) in the Layers palette to make the layer invisible.

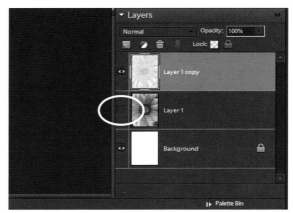

Make Layer 1 invisible.

9. Use the Magic Wand to delete white color from the Layer 1 copy: Select the Magic Wand from the Toolbox at the left. In the Options bar at the top of the screen, set the *tolerance to 70 and uncheck Contiguous*. Position the cursor (which now looks like a magic wand) on an area of white and click. You should see "marching ants" around all the white areas of the image. Press delete to remove only the white, then press Ctrl+D to deselect the selection.

White selected

10. Make Layer 1 visible: Click the eye icon to the left of Layer 1 (the layer with color) to make it visible again.

11. Set the Blend Mode: With the *Layer 1 copy selected* (the layer with the outline effect), choose Multiply from the Blend Mode pull-down menu in the Layers palette.

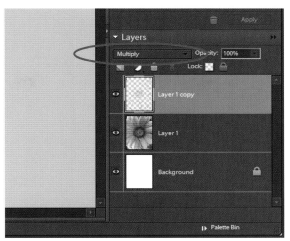

Set the Blend Mode to multiply.

12. Apply the Cutout filter to Layer 1: With *Layer 1* selected, go to **Filter > Artistic > Cutout**. Fit the entire image in the preview window by pressing Ctrl+zero. Set the number of levels to 8, edge simplicity to 0, and edge fidelity to 3. Click OK.

Cutout filter applied to image

13. <u>Apply the Paint Daubs filter to Layer 1</u>: With *Layer 1* selected, go to **Filter > Artistic > Paint Daubs**. Set the brush size to 9, sharpness to 40, and brush type to wide sharp.

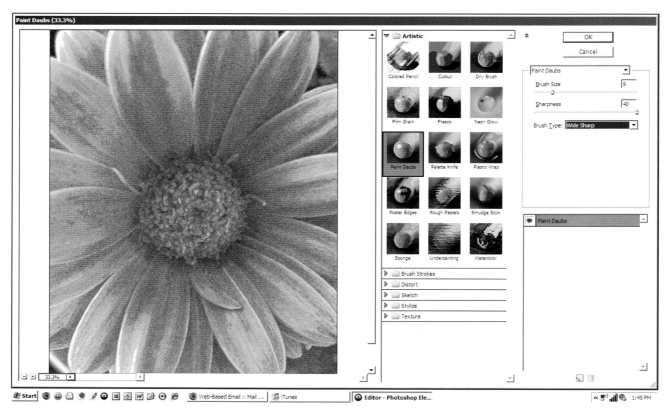

Paint daubs filter applied to image

---

14. <u>Merge the Layer 1 copy and Layer 1</u>: With *Layer 1 copy selected*, go to **Layer > Merge Down** (Ctrl+E). Note: The selected layer is automatically merged with the layer that appears underneath it in the Layers palette. When two layers are merged, the new layer takes the name of the bottom layer (in this case Layer 1).

15. <u>Create a new layer</u>: With *Layer 1 selected* (this is the new, merged image), select all by pressing Ctrl+A. Copy (Ctrl+C) and paste (Ctrl+V). When you paste, Photoshop Elements automatically creates a new layer (Layer 2) for the copied image.

Create a new layer.

NEXT STEPS IN ALTERED PHOTO ARTISTRY

16. <u>Reduce the size of the copied image</u>: With *Layer 2 selected*, open the Free Transform tool by choosing **Image > Transform > Free Transform** (Ctrl+T). Drag a resizing box (any of the empty squares showing in the corners) toward the center to reduce the size of the image.

Use the resizing box to reduce the image size.

17. <u>Position the copied image</u>: Position the cursor in the center of the reduced image (Layer 2) and click and drag it into position above the original (Layer 1). When you are pleased with the juxtaposition, press Enter.

Position copied image in center of original image.

18. <u>Reduce the opacity of Layer 1</u>: Select *Layer 1* (the color layer) and reduce the opacity to 60%–70% by clicking in the Opacity box at the top of the Layers palette and typing a new percentage.

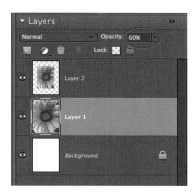

19. <u>Save your work</u>: When you are pleased with the results, go to **File > Save As** (Ctrl+Shift+S) to save the image as a separate file from the original (see Save As, page 7).

Original crocus photo (Crocus.jpg)

Crocus with skewed square-in-a-square

Original pansy (Pansy.jpg)

Pansy composition includes multiple layers to create illusion of depth.

Selective Filtering

The improved selection tools in Photoshop Elements 6 make it easy to create an image that is only partially altered or one that has different effects applied to separate parts of the image.

Original balloon photo (Sky.jpg)

Selectively filtered sky

Instructions

1. <u>Open and optimize the image</u>: See Prepare the Image, page 13, for instructions on opening and optimizing the image. Navigate to Sky.jpg on the CD, select it, and click OK.

2. <u>Duplicate the image once</u>: Make two total copies of the image. Go to **Edit > Duplicate Layer** (Ctrl+J).

3. <u>Choose the Magic Wand</u>: Choose the Magic Wand from the Toolbox on the left.

4. <u>Select a portion of the image</u>: *With Layer 1 selected*, position the cursor, which is now a magic wand, on the sky and click. Hold down the Shift key and repeat as needed until the entire sky is selected.

Select sky.

5. <u>Select and copy the inverse of the selected sky</u>: To select only the balloon, choose **Select > Inverse** (Shift+Ctrl+I). Then copy the balloon by pressing Ctrl+C.

6. <u>Apply the Sponge filter to the sky</u>: Select the sky again by pressing Shift+Ctrl+I. Go to **Filter > Artistic Filters > Sponge**. Set the brush size to 5, definition to 25, smoothness to 1, and click OK.

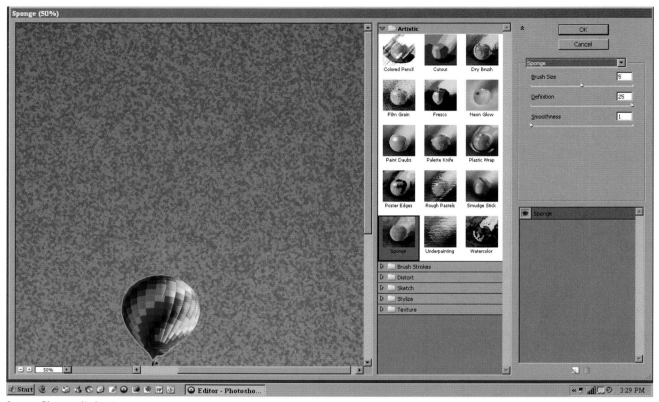

Sponge filter applied to image

7. If you like the result, you can end the exercise here and save your image (see Save As, page 7), or you can continue on with ascending and descending images on page 29.

Ascending and Descending Image Effects

Instructions

1. <u>Paste the image</u>: Paste (Ctrl+V) the balloon (copied during Step 5 of Selective Filtering, page 28) onto the photo. Photoshop Elements automatically creates a new layer for the balloon.

2. <u>Resize the copied balloon</u>: Enlarge the balloon using the Free Transform tool by pressing Ctrl+T. A bounding box will appear around the balloon. Click a corner resizing box and drag outward to enlarge the balloon.

3. <u>Position the image</u>: When the balloon is the desired size, place the cursor in the center and click and drag the balloon into the desired position. Press Enter to apply the changes.

4. <u>To create the illusion of perspective</u>: Change the order of the layers in the Layers palette (see Step 13 of Extracting and Replacing, page 36) so the larger balloon is on top of the smaller balloon.

5. <u>Save your work:</u> When you are pleased with the results, go to **File > Save As** (Ctrl+Shift+S) to save the image as a separate file from the original (see Save As, page 7).

Ascending or descending balloons

You may need to zoom in (Ctrl+plus sign) or out (Ctrl+minus sign) for a better view while resizing.

Impressionist Brush

The Impressionist Brush tool makes it easy to create a painterly look on all, or just a part, of a photographic image.

Original butterfly photo (Butterfly.jpg)

Butterfly with Impressionist Brush

Instructions

1. <u>Open and optimize the image</u>: See Prepare the Image, page 13, for instructions on opening and optimizing the image. Navigate to Butterfly.jpg on the CD, select it, and click OK.

2. <u>Duplicate the image once</u>: Make two total copies of the image. Go to **Edit > Duplicate Layer** (Ctrl+J).

3. <u>Choose the Impressionist tool</u>: Choose the Impressionist tool (the paintbrush with a swirl) from the Toolbox on the left (it may be hidden behind the paintbrush tool).

4. <u>Select the brush settings</u>: From the Options bar at the top of the screen, select a soft-edged brush style, size 60–65, Normal Mode, and 100% opacity.

5. <u>Paint in the background</u>: *With Layer 1 selected*, use the Impressionist Brush to paint in the background. Moving slowly or hovering over a shadow or highlight will allow the brush to develop detail.

Completed background should look similar to this.

6. <u>Reduce the brush size</u>: Reduce the brush size to 35–50. Stroke the outline of the butterfly.

7. <u>Magnify the butterfly</u>: Zoom in on the butterfly by pressing Ctrl+plus sign. Reduce the brush size even further and stroke the details in the center of the butterfly.

8. <u>Adjust the saturation</u>: The finished composition is a little pale, so increase the saturation by adjusting the sliders in the Hue/Saturation dialog box. Go to **Enhance > Adjust Color > Adjust Hue/Saturation** (Ctrl+U) (see Adjusting Color with Hue/Saturation Control, page 50).

Isn't this gerbera daisy luscious? Just imagine how cool it will look when stitched!

The Impressionist Brush can also be applied to portraits. Here is Lori Marquette, my studio partner.

A lovely tangerine rose treated with the Impressionist Brush.

The autumnal colors in these trees are perfect for the Impressionist Brush.

Extracting and Replacing

How often does this happen: Everything is perfect in a photo except for one feature. Maybe the sky is too pale, or the background is too busy, or the point of interest is the wrong color. What to do? Extracting and replacing allows you to replace parts of photos you don't like with parts of photos that you do like. It is a great tool.

Original Garden of the Gods photo (Gods.jpg).

Original Colorado sky photo (Sky.jpg)

The original Garden of the Gods photo is well composed, the light on the rock formations is pretty good, but the sky isn't exciting.

Completed landscape after extracting the sky and replacing it with the Colorado sky photo.

Instructions

1. Open and optimize the image: See Prepare the Image, page 13, for instructions on opening and optimizing the image. Navigate to Gods.jpg on the CD, select it, and click OK.

2. Duplicate the image once: Make two total copies of the image. Go to **Edit > Duplicate Layer** (Ctrl+J).

3. Choose the Magic Wand: Choose the Magic Wand from the Toolbox at the left. In the Options bar across the top of the screen, set the *tolerance to 30 and make sure the Anti-alias and Contiguous boxes are checked*.

The Anti-alias choice smoothes the edge of the selection rather than following the ragged edge of the pixels. When the Contiguous box is checked, only pixels of similar color touching each other are chosen. When the Contiguous box is unchecked, pixels of similar color throughout the photo are chosen.

4. Select a portion of the image: *With Layer 1 selected*, position the cursor, which now looks like a magic wand, in the sky area and click. Most of the sky will be surrounded by "marching ants", indicating the selected area. To add to the selected area, hold down the Shift key, position the wand on the additional area, and click.

If there are still a few small, unselected specks, choose the Selection brush from the Toolbox on the left and use it to clean up the selection. (The Selection brush may be hidden behind the Quick Selection tool.) No need to hold down the Shift key; the brush automatically adds to the selection.

5. Select and copy the inverse: Select the inverse (Shift+Ctrl+I) to switch the selection from the sky to the rocks. Copy the inverse (Ctrl+C), and then close the landscape photo. Don't save any changes you made to the original file in case you'd like to use it for future projects.

6. Create a new document: Go to **File > New > Blank File** (Ctrl+N). In the dialog box, select Transparent from the Background Contents pull-down menu, give the file a unique name, and click OK.

Photoshop Elements automatically measures the size and resolution of the copied portion of the photo and prepares a new document according to those proportions. The grid background in the new window indicates transparency.

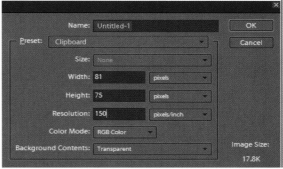

New file dialog box

7. Paste into the new document: Press Ctrl+V to paste the copied rock formations and landscape foreground into the new document.

Pasted rocks

8. Enlarge the canvas: There isn't much room to insert the sky, so to enlarge the canvas, open the Canvas Size dialog box by choosing **Image > Resize > Canvas Size**. In the New Size section, set the height to 9″. Select the bottom center square from the Anchor section to position the image on the enlarged canvas, and click OK.

Paste sky.

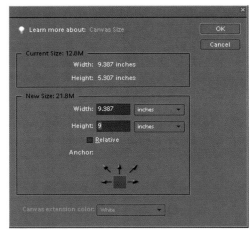

Canvas Size dialog box

9. Open the desired replacement photo: Press Ctrl+O to open the sky photo. Navigate to Sky.jpg on the CD, select it, and click OK.

10. Copy the desired replacement photo: Press Ctrl+A to select the entire sky. You should see "marching ants" around the periphery of the photo. Copy (Ctrl+C) and then close the sky photo.

11. Paste the desired replacement photo: Press Ctrl+V to paste the sky into the landscape. The sky photo is smaller than the landscape photo because it was taken with a lower-resolution camera. In order to fix this discrepancy, we need to resize the sky portion to fit the rest of the landscape.

You may need to zoom in (Ctrl+plus sign) or out (Ctrl+minus sign) for a better view while resizing.

12. Resize the replacement photo using the Free Transform tool: Press Ctrl+T to open the Free Transform tool. A bounding box will appear around the sky photo.

a. Drag upper right: In the Options bar across the top of the screen, make sure the Constrain Proportions box is checked. Click and drag the upper-right resizing box toward the top right corner of the canvas to enlarge the sky proportionally.

Drag upper right.

b. Drag lower left: Click and drag the lower-left resizing box toward the bottom left corner of the canvas. When the sky area is completely full, press Enter to apply the changes. Click and drag the sky photo upward until it is flush with the top of the canvas.

Enlargement complete

13. <u>Rearrange the layers</u>: You'll notice the sky is covering up most of the landscape, but we're going to take care of that now.

Click and drag the sky layer (Layer 2) below the foreground layer (Layer 1). The sky should now appear to be behind the rock formations.

Click and drag the sky layer (Layer 2) below the landscape layer (Layer 1).

14. <u>Adjust the levels</u>: The sky has more contrast between the lightest and darkest areas than the foreground does, making the two look less like they go together. We could reduce the contrast in the sky to make it a little less bright, but why not punch up the foreground instead?

Click the landscape layer (Layer 1) to activate it. Open the Levels dialog box by choosing **Enhance > Adjust Lighting > Levels** (Ctrl+L). Move the center triangle to the right to enhance the midtones to 0.62 and click OK. Now the two images appear as one!

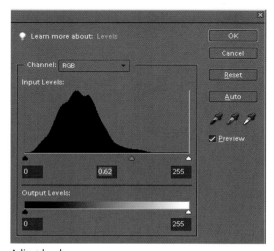

Adjust levels.

Before Levels adjustment

After Levels adjustment

15. <u>Save your work</u>: When you are pleased with the image, go to **File > Save As** (Ctrl+Shift+S) to save the image as a separate file from the original (see Save As, page 7).

Gigi's Iris, 15" × 14"

Georgianne Kandler's altered iris image took on a Japanese block effect when she extracted the background and some inner detail of the iris petals and stem.

Photomerge

Photomerge isn't new to Photoshop Elements, but boy has it been improved! This tool automatically combines multiple photos into one image. Why would we quilters want that? An assembled photo provides a larger image at a higher resolution, so it allows us to enlarge it even more for an Altered Photo quilt before the quality starts breaking down.

Original left section before merge
(Left.jpg)

Original center section before merge
(Center.jpg)

Original right section before merge
(Right.jpg)

Finished Photomerge image

Instructions

1. Open the Photomerge function: Before opening any photos, go to Photomerge by choosing **File > New > Photomerge Panorama.**

2. Choose the files to merge: In the Photomerge dialog box, click the Auto button in the Layout section. In the Source Files section in the center, click the Browse button. Navigate to the CD, and select Left.jpg, Center.jpg, and Right.jpg.

3. Merge the files: When the desired files are visible in the dialog box, click OK.

In a few moments, depending on how many photos there are, how complex they are, and how fast your computer's processor is, the merged image will appear in the workspace. Flatten the merged image by choosing **File > Flatten Image**. You will now have one Background layer that you can fine-tune.

For best results, your photos should be shot with Photomerge in mind so that Photoshop Elements can combine the images seamlessly.

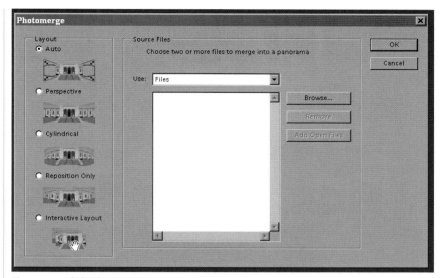

Photomerge dialog box

Merged and flattened image

4. <u>Fine-tune the image with the Clone Stamp tool</u>: The merged and flattened image looks pretty good, except it certainly isn't a rectangle. Select the Clone Stamp tool from the Toolbox on the left (it looks like a rubber stamp). In the Options bar across the top of the screen, select a soft-edged brush, set the size to 450, the Mode to Normal, and the opacity to 100%. Sample an area of the sky that's similar to the area that needs to be cloned by pressing the Alt key and clicking the mouse button. Once sampled, position the brush on the area to be replaced and click and drag as needed. Make sure to clone the sky along the upper edge and the scrubby foliage in the foreground. You may need to select a smaller sized brush for detailed areas. Don't worry if the image has lines; these can be fixed later with the Healing Brush.

5. <u>Smooth the image with the Healing Brush tool</u>: Select the Healing Brush tool from the Toolbox at the left (it looks like a bandage strip). In the Options bar across the top of the screen, set the Mode to Normal and make sure the Sampled button in the Source section is selected. Click on the black triangle to the right of the brush setting to open the drop-down menu. Select a soft-edged brush and set the diameter to 55. Position the brush on an area that has no striations, and sample that portion (Alt+Click). Once sampled, click and drag the brush over the striations. Continue working around the image until all striations are gone.

6. <u>Crop the image</u>: Fit the entire image in the workspace by pressing Ctrl+zero. Crop out the pavement to create a rugged landscape (see Cropping, page 8).

7. <u>Save your work</u>: When you are pleased with the image, go to **File > Save As** (Ctrl+Shift+S) to save the image as a separate file from the original (see Save As, page 7).

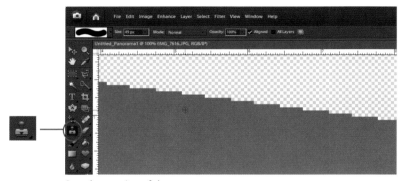
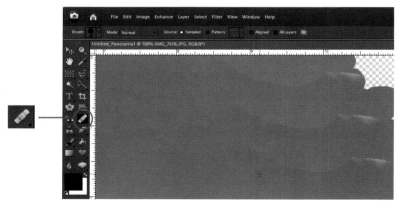

Sample a section of sky.

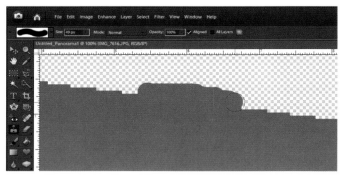

Clone the sky.

Sample a section of sky with no striations.

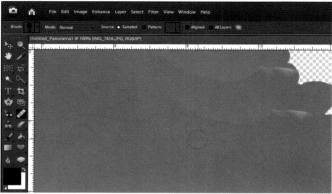

Remove the striations.

Digital Collage

Nothing is quite as exciting and magical for me as digital collage. You can make up a story from bits and pieces of photographs and add a quotation, scripture verse, or greeting for a mixed-media piece that takes little time and has huge impact!

Essentially, digital collage extracts people, places, or things from various sources and puts them together on an electronic canvas to create something entirely different. These three images are separated by thousands of miles and many years, yet together they hint at joyous music echoing through the American Southwest. The photo of singing children is from an early nineteenth-century postcard. I photographed the door at an art museum in Stratford, Ontario, and the rock grotto in a desert outside of Abiquiu, New Mexico.

Sometimes finding just the right image is the biggest challenge of digital collage. I spend lots of time poring through collections of vintage artwork and digital photography, looking for elements that resonate and beg to be combined.

Let's put the children, door, and grotto together in a composition.

Original image of children singing (Children.jpg)

Original door photo (Door.jpg)

Original grotto in rock photo (Grotto.jpg)

Finished digital collage

NEXT STEPS IN ALTERED PHOTO ARTISTRY

Instructions

Extracting the elements is the most time consuming part of digital collage, but Photoshop Elements makes it easier than ever with a variety of selection tools.

1. <u>Open and optimize the image</u>: See Prepare the Image, page 13, for instructions on opening and optimizing the image. Navigate to Door.jpg on the CD, select it, and click OK.

2. <u>Choose the Selection Brush</u>: Choose the Selection Brush from the Toolbox on the left (it may be hidden behind the Quick Selection tool).

3. <u>Select the brush settings</u>: In the Options bar across the top of the screen choose a brush shape, and set the size to 150. Make sure the Selection mode is chosen, and set the hardness to 100%. A hard-edged brush ensures a crisp selection. Remember to reduce the brush size for detailed areas as you work.

4. <u>Make a selection and copy</u>: Click and drag the curser over the entire door shape and surrounding bricks. Take care when selecting the outlining bricks. If you make a mistake, simply press Ctrl+Z to undo your last stroke. Unlike other selection tools, the Selection Brush automatically adds to the selection without the need for the Shift key.

When you are satisfied with the selection, press Ctrl+C to copy it.

5. <u>Paste the selection into a new file</u>: Create a new file (Ctrl+N) with a transparent background. Paste the selection into the new file (Ctrl+V).

6. <u>Save your work</u>: Go to **File > Save As** (Ctrl+Shift+S) and save the file with a unique name (see Save As, page 7). Be sure to **check the Save Transparency box**.

7. <u>Repeat with the other image</u>: Repeat Steps 1–6 with the children photo, paying close attention when selecting the hair, fingers, and space around the legs of the desk.

Assemble the Collage

1. <u>Open the images</u>: Open the *original* rock grotto image (Grotto.jpg on the CD), and the door cutout image one at a time by pressing Ctrl+O. Navigate to wherever each photo is stored, select it, and click OK.

2. <u>Select the image</u>: Select the entire door (Ctrl+A). Close the door cutout window to reveal the original rock grotto.

3. <u>Paste the image</u>: Paste the door cutout on the rock photo (Ctrl+V). Photoshop Elements automatically creates a new layer (Layer 1) containing the door selection.

Paste door on rock.

Selection complete

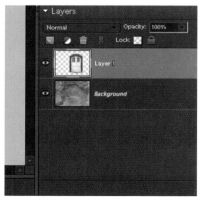

Layers palette

4. <u>Resize the door</u>: The door is out of proportion with the rock grotto, so it will need to be reduced. Open the Free Transform tool by pressing Ctrl+T to resize it.

A bounding box will appear. Click a corner resizing box and drag toward the center of the door to reduce the image. Final size adjustments will be made once all the photos are in place.

5. <u>Open an additional image</u>: Open the children cutout by pressing Ctrl+O. Navigate to wherever it is stored, select it, and click OK.

6. <u>Copy and paste the image</u>: Copy the children cutout by pressing Ctrl+C. Close the file. Paste the image (Ctrl+V) into the image with the rock and door. Photoshop Elements places the children in the middle of the composition, providing a direct size comparison to the door.

Paste children cutout into rock and door.

7. <u>Resize the children</u>: Resize the children so that the boy is just slightly larger than the door, using the Free Transform tool (Ctrl+T).

Resize children.

8. <u>Finalize the positioning</u>: Click and drag the children around in the composition until you are satisfied. Next, move the door: Click on the door layer (Layer 1) and choose the Move tool from the Toolbox at the left. Click and drag the door to the left until the children are not overlapping it.

Blend the Images

The edges of the door and children need to be softened slightly to make them look like they are all part of the same photo, rather than three photos on top of one another.

1. <u>Choose the Smudge tool</u>: Select the Smudge tool (which looks like a white glove) from the Toolbox at the left. It may be hidden behind the Blur tool.

2. <u>Choose a brush</u>: In the Options bar at the top of the screen, choose a brush shape, set the size to 20 pixels, set the Mode to Normal, and strength to 35%. Press Enter to apply the brush settings.

3. <u>Magnify the image</u>: Zoom in on the door by pressing Ctrl+plus sign.

Enlarged image in workspace

4. <u>Smudge</u>: Position the cursor, which now looks like an open circle, on the edge of the doorway—half on and half off. Hold down the mouse button and begin to drag the cursor. The Smudge tool will slightly blur the hard edge of the door outline, softening it and making it look like it's built right into the rock. Because the door is on a separate layer, the smudge will not affect the rock behind the door.

Begin to smudge.

The smudged edges are not a dramatic change, but they certainly make a difference in the way the eye perceives the relationship between the door and the rock.

5. <u>Soften the edges of the children image</u>: Select the layer with the children (Layer 2). There is much more detail in the outline of the children image, so we'll need a considerably smaller brush (12 pixels). Zoom in on the children by pressing Ctrl+plus sign.

Smudge the edges of the children, as you did for the door. This is very precise work, so if the mouse goes astray and smudges something it shouldn't, simply **Undo** (Ctrl+Z) and try again. Avoid smudging the boy's hand and the girl's face.

6. <u>Clone the edges of the children and the door</u>: Select the Clone Stamp tool from the Toolbox on the left. In the Options bar at the top of the screen, choose a soft-edged brush and set the size to 65 pixels and the hardness to 80%.

Before smoothing

Click on the Background layer to select the rock image, and position the cursor on the rock. Sample the colors and textures of the rock by pressing the Alt key and clicking the mouse button.

Click on the layer with the children (Layer 2) and stroke the base around the books, desk legs, and stool. Let's do the same to the base of the door as well. Click the Background layer and sample (Alt+click) another section of rocks near the door. Click on the door layer (Layer 1) and stroke the bottom edge.

After smoothing

7. <u>View the entire image</u>: Press Ctrl+zero and review the entire image.

8. <u>Save your work</u>: When you are pleased with the image, go to **File > Save As** (Ctrl+Shift+S) to save the image as a separate file from the original (see Save As, page 7).

To flatten or not to flatten?

If I was *really* brave and absolutely knew I'd never want to change a thing, I'd flatten the three layers before applying the Clone Stamp tool. However, you never know when a digital image will work for another project with just a little tweak. So, I'm keeping the layers the way they are. That makes sampling and applying the Clone Stamp tool a little more involved, but it's not difficult.

Child clown on a rusty concrete background

Moon on an artificial night sky

Angel on rocks with new sky

Cowgirl on a rocky background and new sky

Virtue by Gale Blair, a digital artist and photographer in central Indiana. She is also the owner of PaperWhimsy. You can reach her at info@paperwhimsy.com and visit her website at www.paperwhimsy.com.

NEXT STEPS IN ALTERED PHOTO ARTISTRY

Working with Color

Adjusting Color with Hue/Saturation Control

Original filtered carnation (Carnation.jpg)

Master (All Colors)

Instructions

1. <u>Open the filtered carnation</u>: Press Ctrl+O to open the carnation image. Navigate to Carnation.jpg on the CD, select it, and click OK.

2. <u>Open the Hue/Saturation dialog box</u>: Go to **Enhance > Adjust Color > Adjust Hue/Saturation**, or press Ctrl+U to open the Hue/Saturation dialog box. The slider bars allow you to adjust hue, saturation, and lightness individually. Note: The default Edit choice is Master, which means you adjust *all* colors in the source image at one time.

3. <u>Adjust the colors</u>: Drag the Hue slider back and forth slowly and watch the colors change. The warm colors are on the right, and the cool colors are on the left.

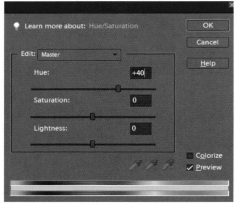

Hue/saturation sliders control overall color changes.

Specific Colors

Stacked under the Master default choice you'll also find controls to adjust the red, yellow, green, cyan, blue, and magenta colors individually.

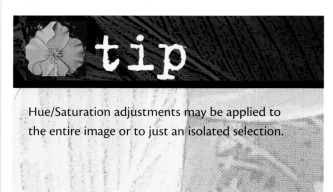

Hue/Saturation adjustments may be applied to the entire image or to just an isolated selection.

Adjusting Color with the Replace Color Tool

In this exercise we'll remove one color and replace it with another.

Instructions

1. Open the filtered carnation: Press Ctrl+O to open the carnation image. Navigate to Carnation.jpg on the CD, select it, and click OK.

2. Open the Replace Color dialog box: Go to **Enhance > Adjust Color > Replace Color**.

Replace Color control panel

3. Sample the image: Select the eyedropper in the upper left corner, position it on the darkest area of the carnation (or whatever color you want to replace), and click the mouse button to take a sample. The boxes in the upper and lower right automatically fill with the selected color.

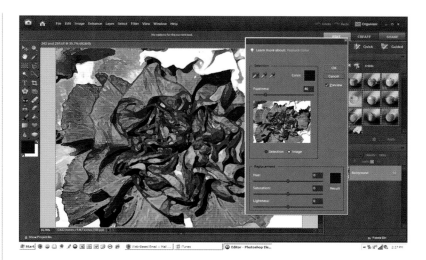

Sample image.

4. Choose a replacement color: Since we don't want to replace the selection with itself, double-click on the Result box at the bottom. A Color Picker dialog box will pop up, allowing you to select a replacement color. Select a color from the rainbow color bar in the middle of the dialog box. The split box at the top right shows the original selected color on the bottom and the new replacement color on the top. Click OK. If the color change doesn't look like what you selected, adjust the Hue and Saturation sliders at the bottom of the original Replace Color dialog box. When you are pleased with the color adjustment, click OK.

Choose replacement color.

Photoshop Elements offers more than one way to change, adjust, or replace color in an image. Experiment and have fun!

The soft posterization of this photo taken in Garden of the Gods, Colorado, (above) is reminiscent of vintage postcards. Fortunately, this effect is not lost when the sky color is replaced (right).

Complex kaleidoscope image of tree against sky

Complex kaleidoscope image responded well to Hue/Saturation adjustment.

Same image adjusted with Replace Color has a very different, but compelling, look.

Converting to Black and White

Converting color images to black and white makes it possible to combine images that don't go together very well in color. There are many ways to convert a color image to black and white in Photoshop Elements, but I like the Hue/Saturation and Remove Color functions best. The advantage of using Hue/Saturation to transform a color image to black and white is that the luminance and lightness are retained.

Carnation image converted to black and white.

Converting via Hue/Saturation

1. Open the filtered carnation: Press Ctrl+O to open the carnation image. Navigate to Carnation.jpg on the CD, select it, and click OK.

2. Open the Hue/Saturation dialog box: Go to **Enhance > Adjust Color > Adjust Hue/Saturation**, or press Ctrl+U.

Hue/Saturation control panel

3. Choose the settings: With Master as the choice in the Edit menu, drag the Saturation slider all the way to the left.

Drag the Saturation slider to the left.

Converting via Remove Color

1. Open the filtered carnation: Press Ctrl+O to open the carnation image. Navigate to Carnation.jpg on the CD, select it, and click OK.

2. Open the Remove Color dialog box: Go to **Enhance > Adjust Color > Remove Color**, or press Shift+Ctrl+U. The Remove Color function automatically converts your color image to grayscale.

3. Adjust the Levels or Brightness/Contrast: To restore rich shadows and detail in the petals, adjust the Levels (Ctrl+L) or Brightness/Contrast (**Enhance > Adjust Lighting > Brightness/Contrast**).

Colorizing

You'll notice a small box at the bottom right of the Hue/Saturation dialog box labeled Colorize. This feature applies color to black-and-white images. When applied selectively, colorizing is a great way to create the look of a vintage, hand tinted photo.

Colorized carnation image

1. <u>Open the filtered carnation:</u> Press Ctrl+O to open the carnation image. Navigate to Carnation.jpg on the CD, select it, and click OK.

2. <u>Remove color:</u> Go to **Enhance > Adjust Color > Remove Color** or press Shift+Ctrl+U to turn the carnation into a black-and-white image.

3. <u>Open the Hue/Saturation dialog box:</u> Go to **Enhance > Adjust Color > Adjust Hue/Saturation** or press Ctrl+U. Click the Colorize box in the lower right corner. Adjust the Hue, Saturation and Lightness sliders until you are satisfied with the result.

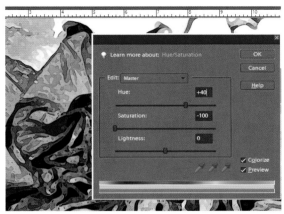

Check the Colorize box in the Hue/Saturation control panel and move the sliders.

4. <u>Save your work:</u> When you are pleased with the image, go to **File > Save As** (Ctrl+Shift+S) to save the image as a separate file from the original (see Save As, page 7).

Additional Examples of Colorize

Photo by Beth Wheeler

In the flower photo above, I only wanted to adjust the color of the blossoms, not the foliage. The Replace Color tool yielded poor results, but the Colorization feature worked wonderfully. If one technique doesn't work well, try another!

Faux Cyanotype

Cyanotype is a photographic process that was discovered in 1842. We can create this aged blue-print look in just a few easy steps.

Original house photo (House.jpg)

Finished house photo with faux cyanotype effect

Instructions

1. <u>Open and optimize the image</u>: See Prepare the Image, page 13, for instructions on opening and optimizing the image. Navigate to House.jpg on the CD, select it, and click OK.

2. <u>Duplicate the image once</u>: Make two total copies of the image. Go to **Edit > Duplicate Layer** (Ctrl+J).

3. <u>Convert to black and white</u>: With Layer 1 selected, go to **Enhance > Adjust Color > Remove Color** (Shift+Ctrl+U) to convert the image to black and white.

4. <u>Increase the contrast</u>: Go to **Enhance > Adjust Lighting > Brightness/Contrast** and increase the contrast by approximately 30%.

5. <u>Apply mezzotint</u>: Go to **Filter > Pixelate > Mezzotint**. Choose fine or medium dots and click OK.

6. Smooth the grainy texture: Go to **Filter > Texture > Grain**. Set the intensity to 7, contrast to 5, and set the grain type to vertical. Click OK.

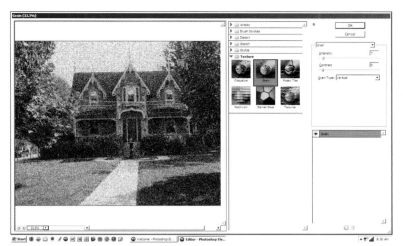

Grain filter dialog box

7. Add the blue-print look: Go to **Enhance > Adjust Color > Color Variations.** With the Midtones button selected and the Amount slider positioned in the middle, click on the image thumbnail above "Increase Blue" twice. Click the image thumbnail above "Decrease Red" once, and click OK.

8. Add a new layer: Press Shift+Ctrl+N to create a new layer (Layer 2). Click and drag the new layer (Layer 2) between the Background layer and Layer 1.

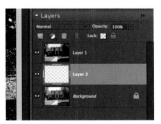

Layer order

9. Fill the layer: With the new layer selected (Layer 2), set the foreground to black and choose the Paint Bucket tool from the Toolbox. Position the Paint Bucket cursor anywhere on the photo and click. You won't see anything happen on the photo, but the layer thumbnail in the Layers palette will fill with black.

Filled layer

10. Add an optional border: With the cyanotype layer (Layer 1) selected, use the Rectangular Selection tool to select all but a tiny border around the image. Invert the selection (Shift+Ctrl+I) and delete it. Press Ctrl+D to deselect the border. For a grunge border, select the Eraser tool from the Toolbox at the left. In the Options bar across the top of the screen, select a dry brush shape, set the size to 25, the mode to brush, and the opacity to 100%. Click and drag the Eraser tool along the border of the photo to create a rough edge.

11. Save your work: When you are pleased with the image, go to **File > Save As** (Ctrl+Shift+S) to save the image as a separate file from the original (see Save As, page 7).

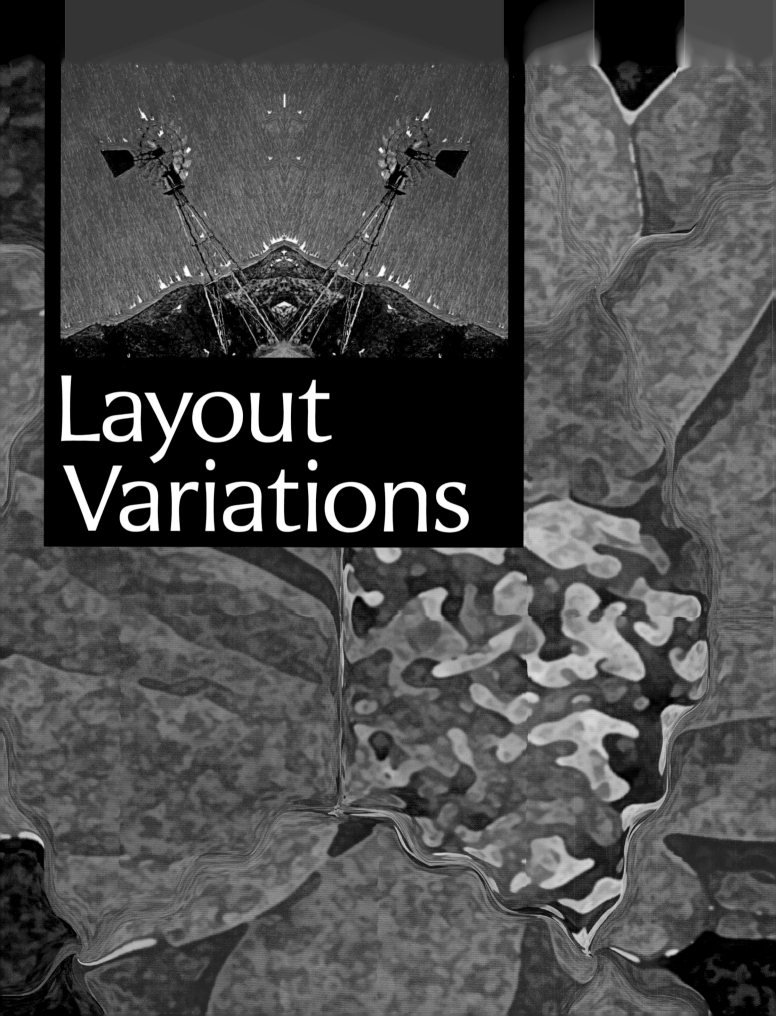

Layout
Variations

Repeating Images

Repeating an image creates a visual rhythm that moves beyond the image itself, so that the image becomes more than the sum of its parts.

Mirror images, linear repetitions, reflected images, and petal arrangements are just a few examples of repeated images. Photoshop Elements makes it easy to accomplish these layout variations.

Photo by Beth Wheeler

Original Geronimos photo (Geronimos.jpg)

I took this photo in Geronimos, a monastery outside Lisbon in Portugal. It has become a favorite design motif and frequently appears in my digital collage and art quilts.

Mirror Images

Reminiscent of early stereoscopic photos, a mirrored image is simply a reflected copy of the image next to the original. There is something graphically powerful in the pair. Strong natural light from the center courtyard sets the stage for an easy mirror image composition.

Finished mirror image

1. Open and optimize the image: See Prepare the Image, page 13, for instructions on opening and optimizing the image. Navigate to Geronimos.jpg on the CD, select it, and click OK.

2. Copy and paste the image: Press Ctrl+A to select the entire image, and then press Ctrl+C to copy the image. Open a new document (Ctrl+N) and paste (Ctrl+V) the copied image into it.

3. Flip the image: Go to **Image > Rotate > Flip Horizontally** to flip the image horizontally. Press Ctrl+A to select the entire image, and then press Ctrl+C to copy the image.

4. Enlarge the canvas: Select the original Geronimos.jpg image from Step 1 and go to **Image > Resize > Canvas Size**. Anchor the existing photo to the left center and set the width to twice the original size. Click OK.

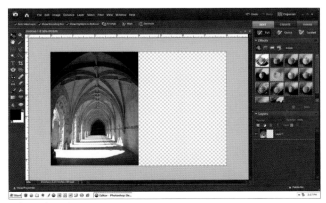

Enlarged canvas.

5. Paste the flipped image to the enlarged canvas: Paste (Ctrl+V) the flipped image onto the enlarged canvas. Photoshop Elements will place the copy in the center of the canvas. Choose the Move tool from the Toolbox on the left, and drag the image into place. Flatten the layers by choosing **Layer > Flatten Image**.

6. Save your work: When you are pleased with the image, go to **File > Save As** (Ctrl+Shift+S) to save the image as a separate file from the original (see Save As, page 7).

7. Finishing touches: If there are any white lines at the center seam, they can be eliminated with the Clone Stamp tool (see Step 4, page 40).

Linear Repetitions

A linear repetition of images can be made in the same manner as Mirror Images, page 59, except that you don't need to flip the copied image. Simply enlarge the canvas width (**Image > Resize > Canvas Size**), copy (Ctrl+C), paste (Ctrl+V), and arrange the copied image as many times as you want it to appear in your linear repetition.

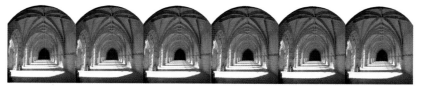

The repetition of the center hallway and strong shadows creates a unified pattern.

Reflected Linear Repetitions

Once you have created a linear repetition of an image, you can reflect it either horizontally or vertically. First flatten the layers by choosing **Layer > Flatten Image**. Press Ctrl+A to select the entire image, and then press Ctrl+C to copy the image.

Enlarge your canvas by choosing **Image > Resize > Canvas Size** and increase the canvas height to twice the original size. Paste (Ctrl+V) the copied image.

Reflect the copied image vertically by choosing **Image > Rotate > Flip Layer Vertical**. Arrange the reflected copy and flatten the image when finished (**Layer > Flatten Image**). To position the entire image vertically, go to **Image > Rotate > 90° Left**.

Horizontal reflected linear image

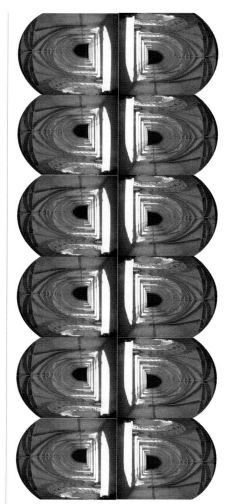

Vertical reflected linear image

The area where the shadows intersect creates a diamond shape that is more prominent in the vertical arrangement than in the horizontal.

Petal Arrangement

A petal arrangement can be achieved by copying (Ctrl+C) and pasting (Ctrl+V) the original image three times (for a total of four images) and rotating copy one 90°, copy two 180°, and copy three 270°.

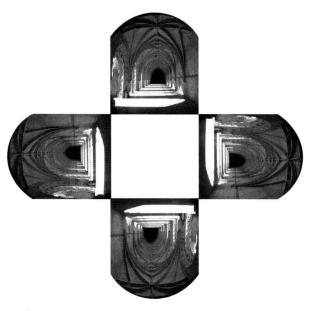

4-petal arrangement

8-petal arrangement

Repeating the same image requires a lot from your computer. Before beginning a complex layout, here are a few tips:

- Start or restart the computer and open Photoshop Elements only. Avoid opening any other applications or windows.

- When experimenting, use a low-resolution image to work out the desired arrangement. Save only the one you like best and discard all the rest. Then, re-create the favored layout using the high-resolution image.

- Convert the image to black and white to reduce the file size and make manipulation less memory hungry.

Four-Way Design

Another way to create secondary designs is to place four copies of the image at intersecting angles.

Original windmill photo (Windmill.jpg)

Finished windmill

I took a photo of this creaky windmill along a long, bumpy, unpaved road on the way to Tent Rocks National Monument outside of Santa Fe, New Mexico.

Instructions

1. <u>Open and optimize the image</u>: See Prepare the Image, page 13, for instructions on opening and optimizing the image. Navigate to Windmill.jpg on the CD, select it, and click OK.

2. <u>Increase the saturation</u>: Go to **Enhance > Adjust Color > Adjust Hue/ Saturation**, or press Ctrl+U. Increase the saturation approximately 40% by adjusting the slider bar.

Adjust saturation.

3. <u>Enlarge the canvas</u>: Go to **Image > Resize > Canvas Size**. Enlarge the canvas to 16" wide × 13.5" tall, with the photo anchored in the bottom center.

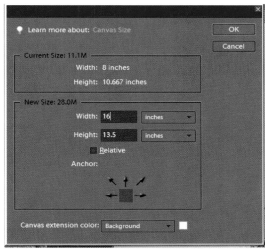

Canvas Size dialog box

4. <u>Clone the sky</u>. Review Step 4 of the Photomerge section (page 40) for more information on cloning. Use the Clone Stamp tool to extend the sky to the top, right and left edges of the enlarged canvas.

Windmill with cloned sky in progress

5. <u>Rotate the canvas</u>: Go to **Image > Rotate > Custom**. Set the angle to 45°, select the Left button, and click OK.

6. <u>Choose the Marquee tool</u>: Select the Marquee tool from the Toolbox at the left. In the Options bar at the top of the screen, choose Fixed Size from the Mode menu and set the size to 8" wide × 10.5" tall. Click on the windmill image to activate the marquee. Click and drag the marquee so that the windmill base is placed in the bottom right corner with no white background included in the selection.

7. <u>Copy and paste the selection</u>: Copy (Ctrl+C) the selection. Open a new document (Ctrl+N) and place (Ctrl+V) the selection into it. Close the original windmill image (Windmill.jpg), making sure not to save any of the changes made to it.

8. <u>Apply desired filters or brushes (optional)</u>: Alter the photo using your choice of filters or brushes. I used the Pattern Stamp tool, which gave the image a painted texture.

Windmill altered with pattern stamp

9. <u>Save your work:</u> When you are pleased with the image, go to **File > Save As** (Ctrl+Shift+S) to save the image as a separate file from the original (see Save As, page 7). Don't close the file.

10. <u>Make a Layer and Copy it:</u> *With your newly saved file still open*, double-click on Background in the Layers palette to turn it into a layer. Keep the name as Layer 0 and click OK. Press Ctrl+A to select all of Layer 0, then Ctrl+C to copy it. Press Ctrl+D to deselect Layer 0.

11. <u>Enlarge the canvas:</u> Go to **Image > Resize > Canvas Size**. Increase the canvas size to double the height and double the width, with the image anchored in the upper left-hand corner. Press Ctrl+0 to fit the entire image on the screen.

12. <u>Paste, flip, and position the image:</u> Paste (Ctrl+V) the copied Layer 0 onto the enlarged canvas. This will be Layer 1. *With Layer 1 selected*, go to **Image > Rotate > Flip Layer Horizontal**. Click and drag the flipped Layer 1 to the upper right-hand corner of the canvas.

13. <u>Merge the layers:</u> *With Layer 1 selected*, go to **Layer > Merge Visible** to merge Layer 0 with Layer 1.

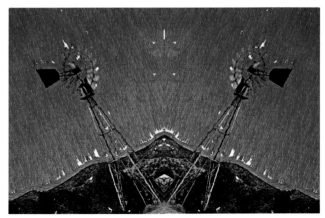

Merged Layer 0 and Layer 1

14. <u>Duplicate Layer 1:</u> Press Ctrl+J to duplicate the merged Layer 1. This will be Layer 1 copy.

15. <u>Flip and position Layer 1 copy:</u> *With Layer 1 copy selected*, Go to **Image > Rotate > Flip Layer Vertical**. Click and drag the flipped Layer 1 copy to fill the bottom half of the canvas.

16. <u>Flatten and repair:</u> Flatten the image by choosing **Layer > Flatten Image**. Repair any white areas at the seams with the Clone Stamp tool. Review Step 4 of the Photomerge section (page 40) for more information on cloning.

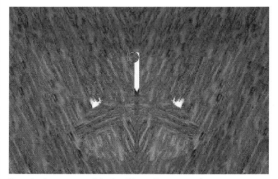

Repair the seams with the Clone Stamp tool.

17. <u>Save your work:</u> When you are pleased with the image, go to **File > Save As** (Ctrl+Shift+S) to save the image as a separate file from the original (see Save As, page 7).

Banner Layout

Using the techniques shown in Repeating Images (page 59), it's easy to create banner layouts for scarves, borders, and other vertical or horizontal compositions. Below are a few examples of border layouts using the same altered pansies image.

Original altered pansies image (Altered_Pansies.jpg)

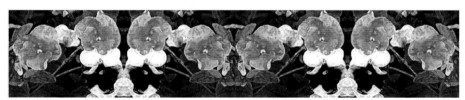

End-to-end horizontal banner was achieved by copying and pasting mirrored pairs of the original.

End-to-end vertical banner

Abstraction

Almost any tool, filter, or effect in Photoshop Elements can be used to create an abstract image. Use the settings with the greatest degree of change and apply it more than once, or apply one effect on top of another!

The capability of Photoshop Elements to resize, copy, paste, rotate, and transform images opens new horizons in layout, as well as image manipulation. Here are just

Transform Tools

There are several powerful tools for transforming your images: Skew, Distort, Perspective, and Free Transform.

Original red lily photo (Lily.jpg)

Instructions

1. <u>Open and optimize the image</u>: See Prepare the Image, page 13, for instructions on opening and optimizing the image. Navigate to Lily.jpg on the CD, select it, and click OK.

2. <u>Duplicate the image</u>: Make two total copies of the image. Go to **Edit > Duplicate Layer** (Ctrl+J). Photoshop Elements doesn't allow certain changes to be applied to the Background layer, so all tools will be used on the duplicate layer (Layer 1).

3. <u>Enlarge the canvas</u>: Go to **Image > Resize > Canvas Size**. Increase the height and width to double their original size, position the square in the center of the anchor section, and click OK.

4. <u>Transform the image</u>: Go to **Image > Transform** and apply either the Skew, Distort, Perspective, or Free Transform tool from the pop-up menu. When you select one of the Transform tools, a bounding box will appear with resizing boxes at each corner. Experiment by dragging the resizing boxes to see how each tool will affect your image.

5. <u>Save your work</u>: When you are pleased with the image, go to **File > Save As** (Ctrl+Shift+S) to save the image as a separate file from the original (see Save As, page 7).

A Closer Look at Transform Tools

SKEW

Go to **Image > Transform > Skew**.

Drag left.

Drag right.

DISTORT

Go to **Image > Transform > Distort**.

Drag straight up.

Drag straight down.

PERSPECTIVE

Go to **Image > Transform > Perspective**. Notice that this tool moves not only the corner you grasp but the adjacent corner as well.

Drag left.

Drag straight down.

FREE TRANSFORM

Go to **Image > Transform > Free Transform**. Notice that this tool moves three corners at once. Hold down the Control key while dragging a resizing box to move just one corner at a time.

Drag straight up.

Drag straight down.

Distortion Filters

The Distortion filters are located in **Filter > Distort**.

A brief sample of each one is below.

Displacement Map

Displacement maps are distortion filters that can be installed into Photoshop Elements as add-ons. I've included some of my favorite displacement maps on the CD. For more information on loading and using displacement maps, see the text document (Install_Addons.doc) on the CD.

Displacement map 5 (APA_Map5.psd)

The settings for this effect were:

HORIZONTAL SCALE: 30

VERTICAL SCALE: 30

DISPLACEMENT MAP: Stretch to fit

UNDEFINED AREAS: Wrap around

Glass

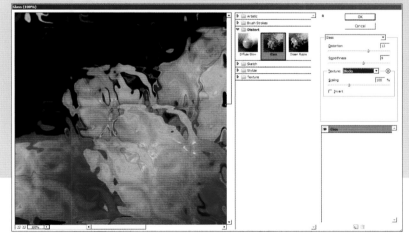

Glass distortion

The settings for this effect were:

DISTORTION: 13

SMOOTHNESS: 9

TEXTURE: Blocks

SCALING: 100%

Not inverted

Ocean Ripple

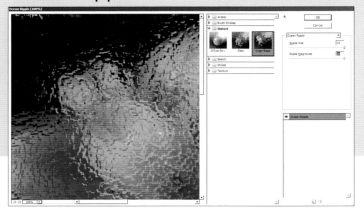

The settings for this effect were:

RIPPLE SIZE: 15

RIPPLE MAGNITUDE: 20

Ocean ripple distortion

Liquify

The settings for this effect were:

BRUSH SIZE: 370

BRUSH PRESSURE: 50

TURBULENT JITTER: 70

Liquify distortion. Click and drag the curser on your image to activate this filter. How fun!

Zigzag

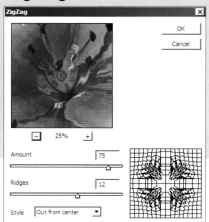

The settings for this effect were:

AMOUNT: 75

RIDGES: 12

STYLE: Out from center

Zigzag distortion

NEXT STEPS IN ALTERED PHOTO ARTISTRY

Wave

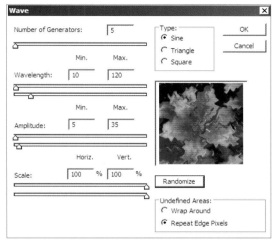

One variation of the Wave distortion created by clicking the Randomize button below the image preview window.

Pinch

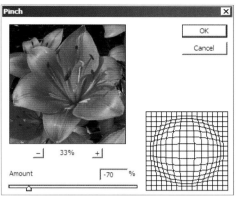

Pinch distortion -70. This would be a great filter to use for placing an image on a cylindrical object, such as a vase or glass.

Ripple Effect

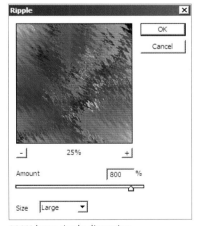

800% large ripple distortion

Shear

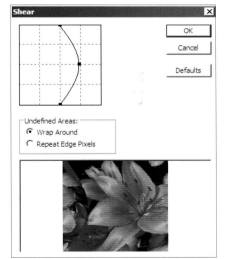

Shear with arc center point pulled to the right and wrap around applied

Polar Coordinates

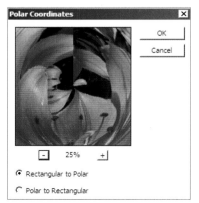

Rectangular-to-polar coordinates

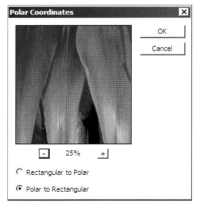

Polar-to-rectangular coordinates

Spherize

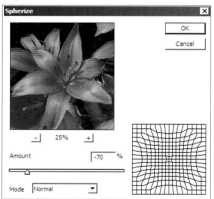

Normal mode, amount set to -70 (concave)

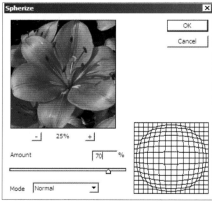

Normal mode, amount set to +70 (convex)

Twirl

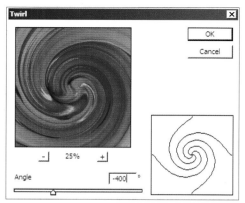

Twirl angle set to -400; photo appears to swirl in one direction.

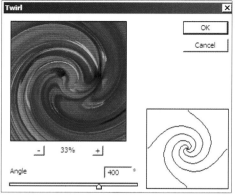

Twirl angle set to +400; photo appears to swirl in opposite direction.

Tropical Sunset began as a photo of the sunset in my backyard—really! Zigzag filter was applied, then Hue and Saturation were adjusted.

Orange turquoise whirl

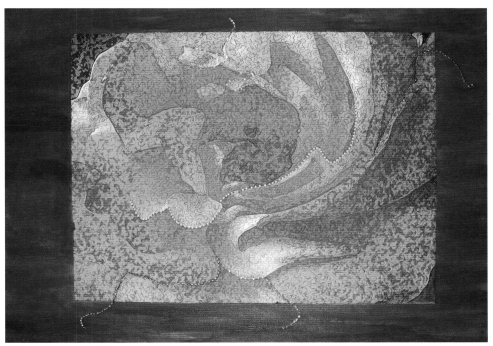

Whirlwind began as a photo of a pink rose blossom. Zigzag filter was applied to change the motion of the petal arrangement.

Pink/magenta rose whirl

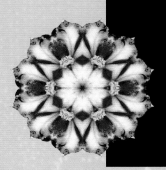

Embellishments

After you alter your photos, you may want to print them on pretreated fabric, embellish them with thread painting or beads and buttons, and mount your finished piece. There are many options for embellishments. Experiment and have fun!

See Book 1, *Altered Photo Artistry*, for the following topics:

Adding Thread Details:

- Preparing for Stitching
- Making an Outline Map
- Outline Stitching
- Filling in with Texture
- Filling in with Color

- Finishing
- Fun Projects: book covers, postcards, greeting cards, friendship books, tote bags, and pillow shams

Rubber Stamps

Rubber stamps and ink or paint for fabric make it easy to add texture and words to your work, increasing the appearance of layers and complexity.

Yarns and Ribbons

All of the interesting fibers, yarns, and ribbons in craft and needlework stores call out to be used for couching and embroidery. Experiment with them all!

Fibers and ribbons

Beads and Baubles

Designwise, I am an all-or-nothing girl. Either the design is embellished to the max ("Nothing succeeds like excess."), or it's quite clean and devoid of baubles. I freely admit to being distracted by bright, shiny things and hoarding beads by the bundle in my studio.

Manufacturers offer an array of inks and stamps that are perfect for working on fabric.

gallery

Protea (before)

Protea and Old Lace (after), 13" × 17", by Diane Harman-Hoog of www.quiltersthreads.com.

Theotokos (God Bearer), 15″ × 18″, by Ruthann Logsdon Zaroff, Belleville, Michigan. Quilt interpretation of Eastern Orthodox icon.

Christ Pantokrator (Christ Almighty), 9½″ × 18″, by Ruthann Logsdon Zaroff, Belleville, Michigan. Eastern Orthodox icon, dating from about 800 A.D. The original resides at St. Catherine's Monastery in the Sinai.

Fire! 17″ × 22″, by Priscilla Stultz, Fairfax, Virginia. The composition is a result of an online workshop with the author. The inspiration was taken from personal photos, which the quilter manipulated in Photoshop Elements and printed on fabric.

Two Rosebuds, 9½″ × 16″, by Sherry Lidgard, Ocean Springs, Mississippi.

Colorful Conversations, 15″ × 21″, by Libberata Toscano, Villeneuve, Switzerland. Libbi took the original photo in 1999 at the Singapore Bird Park.

Glowy Joey, 18″ × 24″, by Bridget Lilja. Bridget adjusted the image and ended up with a photo that looked as if it were glowing from within. After printing and stitching the four panels together, she attached a hand-dyed border, quilted the piece with variegated threads, and added some hot-fix crystals to give it a bit of sparkle.

Essence, 21″ × 29″, by Wen Redmond.

Knockout Rose, 8½″ × 10½″, by Jane Chandler, Bloomington, Indiana.

Yellow Trumpets, 26″ × 22″, by Dana Lynch.

About the Author

BETH WHEELER a.k.a. "Muttonhead," is a freelance artist, product-development specialist, author, and teacher. In the past eighteen years, she has written more than 45 books for sewing, quilting, craft, and collecting audiences; hundreds of articles for trade and consumer publications; and published her own line of Muttonhead quilting patterns and products. Beth has been a crafter since age five and a quilter since age sixteen. She credits her mother and maternal grandmother with the inspiration and the introduction to early techniques—and access to a Singer featherweight.

A passion for discovery led her to develop processes for analysis of technique and design. These skills are the basis for her classes, workshops, articles, books, and products.

Beth lives in northern Indiana with her husband, Geoffrey; son, Jake; and dogs, Elsie and Sydney, in a house happily crowded with a jumble of fabrics, computers, printers, projects in progress, and treasured "stuff" too precious to actually use.

Also by Beth Wheeler:

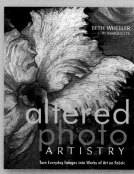

Resources

PHOTO-EDITING SOFTWARE

Adobe Photoshop Elements 6

Adobe Systems Incorporated
www.adobe.com

Free 30-day trial version of Adobe's Photoshop Elements for PC or Mac computers

INSPIRATIONAL DIGITAL ART WEBSITES

Gale Blair
www.paperwhimsy.com

Maggie Taylor
www.maggietaylor.com

BETH'S ONLINE CLASSES

www.quilterskeeplearning.com

Classes include Altered Photo Artistry, More Altered Photo Artistry, Altered Portraits, Beginning Photoshop Elements, Intermediate Photoshop Elements, and Joy of Rust-Dyeing

BOOKS FOR FURTHER READING

Photoshop Elements 6 for Dummies,
by Barbara Obermeier and Ted Padova,
from Wiley Publishing, 2008

Photoshop Fine Art Effects Cookbook,
by John Beardsworth,
from O'Reilly Publishing, 2006

Photoshop Blending Modes Cookbook for Digital Photographers,
by John Beardsworth,
from O'Reilly Publishing, 2005

The Photoshop Elements 6 Book for Digital Photographers,
by Scott Kelby and Matt Kloskowski,
from New Riders Press, 2008

Adobe Photoshop CS3 Classroom in a Book,
by Adobe Creative Team,
from Adobe Press, 2007

Photoshop Elements 6: The Missing Manual,
by Barbara Brundage,
from Pogue Press, 2007

Digital Essentials: The Quilt Maker's Must-Have Guide to Images, Files, and More!
by Gloria Hansen,
from Electric Quilt, 2008

Digital Art Studio, by Karin Schminke, Dorothy Simpson Krause, and Bonny Pierce Lhotka,
from Watson Guptill Publications, 2004

TOOLS AND SUPPLIES

Kaleidoscope Kreator from Kaleidoscope Collections, LLC
www.kalcollections.com

Software for creating beautiful kaleidoscope images from your own photos; free trial version available as a download.

Dharma Trading Company
www.dharmatrading.com

Fabrics, blanks, chemicals, dyes, and much more

PHOTOSHOP PLUG-IN FOR RESIZING

Genuine Fractals
www.ononesoftware.com

Great Titles *from* C&T PUBLISHING

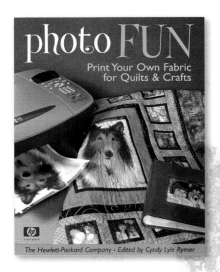

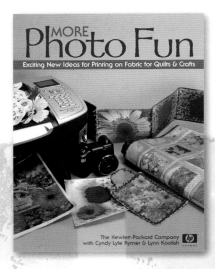

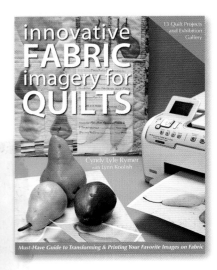

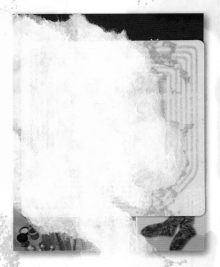

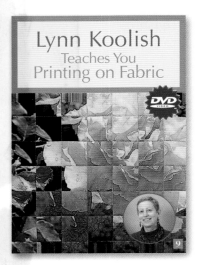

Available at your local retailer or **www.ctpub.com** *or* **800.284.1114**

For a list of other fine books from C&T Publishing,
ask for a free catalog:

C&T PUBLISHING, INC.

P.O. Box 1456
Lafayette, CA 94549
(800) 284-1114

Email: ctinfo@ctpub.com
Website: www.ctpub.com

C&T Publishing's professional photography services are now available
to the public. Visit us at www.ctmediaservices.com.

For quilting supplies:

COTTON PATCH

1025 Brown Ave.
Lafayette, CA 94549
Store: (925) 284-1177
Mail order: (925) 283-7883

Email: CottonPa@aol.com
Website: www.quiltusa.com

Note: Fabrics used in the quilts shown may not be currently
available, as fabric manufacturers keep most fabrics in
print for only a short time.